Copycat Recipes

The Ultimate Cookbook to Replicate Your Favorite American Fast-Food Dishes at Home

Chris McDony

Tables of Contents

—

Introduction

I would like to thank and congratulate you for getting this book, Copycat Recipes.
People all over the world love to eat, enjoy and relax, especially in western countries. People love to go to restaurants to eat with their families, friends, and loved ones.

Whether you are a child or an adult, eating fast food outdoors has become a fast-growing trend. It is delicious and easy for everyone to enjoy. Many fast-food restaurants are opening all over the world due to the increasing demand of people.

Nowadays, hamburgers are people's go-to for fast food. If you live in America, you will know the value of burgers. It would not be wrong to say that America is the nation of burgers.
What if I told you that you can enjoy the famous fast-food dishes in the comfort of your own home?
Isn't that great?

Copied recipes truly inspire home cooking! Whether you are cooking for the whole family or entertaining with colleagues and friends. By following a copycat recipe, you will be able to serve an unforgettable meal that will bring joy to your family and friends.
This book mainly focuses on providing you with the replica recipes of the famous fast foods served all over the world by different fast-food restaurants.
Enjoy it!

Chapter 1: Hamburgers

1. McDonalds Double Cheeseburger

Preparation time: 20 minutes

Servings: 1

Difficulty: Moderate

Ingredients:

- A quarter lb. of ground beef
- One plain burger bun
- Half teaspoon of diced onion
- Two slices of American cheese
- One dill pickle
- One tablespoon of ketchup
- Half teaspoon of American mustard (French's mustard)
- Two teaspoons of boiling water
- Salt

Instructions:

1. The ground beef can be divided into two even halves. Roll each piece of ground beef into a ball and press them flat on waxed paper until they are around 1/8-inch-thick for each patty.

2. In a dry frying pan over medium to hot heat, cut the burger bun in half and gently toast each bun's inner face.

3. Remove the buns and cook roughly 2 minutes per side of each burger patty in the pan. Lightly salt each patty during cooking.

4. Put the first patty on the bottom bun, followed by a slice of American cheese. Then put the second burger patty on top, followed by another slice of cheese.

5. Top the burgers with two slices of dill pickle, then the diced onion.

6. Spread ketchup and French's Mustard on the top bun and place on top of the burger stack.

7. Microwave the whole double cheeseburger (including the bun) for 15 seconds.

2. McDonald's Vegan Big Mac

Preparation time: 20 minutes

Servings: 4

Difficulty: Easy

Ingredients:

- Eight Vegan Burgers
- Eight slices Vegan Cheese
- Four large Burger Rolls
- Two large Gherkins
- Two tablespoons Minced White Onion
- Half a Baby Gem Lettuce

For the vegan Big Mac Sauce

- Three tablespoons Vegan Mayonnaise
- One teaspoon of Garlic Powder
- One teaspoon of Onion Powder
- Two teaspoons of Yellow Mustard
- One teaspoon of White Wine Vinegar
- Two teaspoons of paprika

Instructions:

1. Firstly, prepare the sauce by mixing all of the Vegan Big Mac Sauce ingredients in a mixing bowl.

2. If you bought thick vegan burger patties, slice them in half lengthwise to make two thinner patties. If the patties are already thin, skip this stage.

3. Then place the burgers in the oven, and follow the packet's instructions to ensure you cook them well.

4. Dice the onion into small pieces.

5. Slice the gherkins into thin circles.

6. Slice the lettuce, then shred into thin strips.

7. Now take your burger buns and very carefully cut them into three pieces. If the buns are too thin to slice into three. Use another bottom half of a bun as the middle bun.

8. Spread the Vegan Big Mac sauce you prepared earlier onto the sliced bread rolls, top and bottom.

9. Start building your burger by arranging the lettuce, onions then gherkins on the bun in that order.

10. To give the cheese time to melt, place them on the burger patties in the oven two minutes before the burger patties should come out of the oven.

11. Take the patties out of the oven and complete your burgers.

12. Enjoy!

3. Burger King Big King

Preparation time: 30 minutes

Servings: 4

Difficulty: Easy

Ingredients:

- 1/4 cup mayonnaise
- Two teaspoons of French dressing
- One teaspoon white vinegar
- Half teaspoon granulated sugar
- One and a half teaspoons sweet pickle relish
- Four burger buns
- One and a half pounds ground beef
- Eight slices of American cheese
- One and one-third cups shredded lettuce
- Two white onion
- Eight dill pickle slices
- One pinch of salt and pepper

Instructions:

1. Begin with the sauce being cooked. In a small cup, mix all the sauce ingredients, and refrigerate until desired.
2. Chop down some of the white onion slices and set them aside.
3. Preheat the gas grill to a high temperature.

4. Divide the ground beef into eight equal portions when preheating your grill. Press each flat patty. Use this bun as a reference for rough size, ensuring that the patties are of comparable size.

5. On either side, grill the patties for 3 minutes, and season as you take them off the grill.

6. Lightly toast the buns either on the grill or in a toaster when you are cooking the patties.

7. Make your burger in the following order, after it has been cooked; Patty-Cheese-Patty-Cheese-Onion Rings-Pickle Slices-Sauce.

8. A top tip is to send a blast in the microwave for 15 seconds to the constructed burgers!

4. Burger King Rodeo Burger

Preparation time: 30 minutes

Servings: 6

Difficulty: Moderate

Ingredients:

- Two lbs. lean ground hamburger
- Half teaspoon garlic powder
- 1/4 teaspoon of salt
- 1/4 teaspoon of pepper
- 1/4 teaspoon of onion powder
- Six slices of American cheese
- Six large Alexia onion rings
- Six pretzel buns

Instructions:

1. Heat the grill to a medium-high temperature.
2. Put the hamburger, garlic powder, salt, pepper and onion powder in a broad mixing bowl. Section the mixture into six patties.
3. Place the burgers on the grill or in a saucepan and cook for 5-6 minutes. Turnover and cook for an extra 3-4 minutes or until required. For medium burgers, the internal temperature should be 145-150 degrees F, and the medium well should be 150-165. Cover the burgers with a slice of

cheese and let them melt. Remove the buns from the burgers and finish with B.B.Q. Sauce and an onion ring.

5. T.G.I. Friday's Jack Daniels Burger

Preparation time: 1 hour 45 minutes

Servings: 6

Difficulty: Moderate

Ingredients:

Glaze

- One cup of water
- One and a half cups of pineapple juice
- Half cup of teriyaki sauce
- Two tablespoons soy sauce
- Two cups of brown sugar
- ¼ cup lemon juice
- ¼ cup white onion, finely minced
- 1/4 cup Jack Daniels Whiskey
- Three cloves garlic, minced
- ¼ teaspoon cayenne pepper

Burger

- Two pounds of ground sirloin (or other ground beef, with around 20% fat)
- Kosher salt and black pepper, to taste
- Six slices of white Cheddar or provolone cheese
- 12 slices bacon (about half of a one-pound package)
- Six hamburger buns
- One tomato, sliced

- One red onion, sliced
- Six large leaves of lettuce
- Hamburger pickle chips

Instructions:

For Glaze

1. Mix the water, pineapple juice, teriyaki sauce, soy sauce, and brown sugar in a wide saucepan over medium heat. Bring to a gentle boil, stirring regularly, and then drop to a medium simmer immediately. To mix, add the remaining glaze ingredients and stir.

2. Let the mixture boil for about an hour, or until syrupy and halved. If you can prevent it, don't turn up the flame; low heat is sufficient without burning the sugar to create the perfect glaze. Be careful not to cause the glaze to boil.

Burgers

1. Divide the ground sirloin into six evenly sized sections. They should be about the size of tennis balls.

2. Round each ball out softly, and then flatten each ball to build your patty. You want to be
   sure, that you do all of this very gently because you don't want the meat to be over-handled.

3. To make a small indent, softly press your thumb into the middle of each patty. This will keep the burgers from bloating while they cook, so when grilling, you will not have

---

to flatten them. Season with pepper and salt and put aside when the bacon is being cooked.

4. Cover an aluminum foil baking tray and line up the bacon on top. The bacon will be close, but you don't want it to overlap. Two pans may have to be used.

5. In the cold oven, place the pan or pans and then heat them to 400 ° F.

6. Check your bacon after 17 minutes. Take it out if it is completely crispy. If not, until it is done, check every 3 minutes. Transfer the bacon to a plate lined with paper towels to absorb excess oil.

7. Preheat to a high temperature on the grill. Place the burgers on the hottest part of the grill when it is ready.

8. You will notice the juices after 5 minutes or so as they begin to fill the divots at the top of your burger. This means the meat in the middle is cooking, and they should be ready to flip.

9. Gently use a basting brush to flip the burgers and grill for about a minute before brushing on the Jack Daniels glaze. Let it cook for another 2 minutes, then add the cheese to the top. Close the lid on the burger to melt the Provolone cheese. You're ready to serve the burger when the cheese is melted (it should only take a minute or so).

10. Check with an instant-read thermometer if you're not sure your burgers are done.

11. As you toast the buns, let the burgers sit. Then, add a little extra glaze to the bottom of each bun, then add the burger and all the fixings you like! Immediately serve.

6. Wendy's Bacon Portabella Mushroom Melt

Preparation time: 40 minutes

Servings: 2

Difficulty: Moderate

Ingredients:

Burger

- 14 oz. lean ground beef
- One teaspoon of seasoning salt, steak spice, or to taste
- Six cremini mushrooms, sliced
- One tablespoon of butter plus more for buttering the buns
- Six strips applewood smoked bacon, cooked crisp
- Four cheddar cheese slices
- Two brioche buns
- Salt and pepper to taste
- Cheese Sauce
- Two tablespoons of butter
- One cup of aged cheddar cheese, grated
- Two tablespoons of flour
- One cup of milk
- Salt to taste
- pinch of cayenne

Instructions:

1. With the beef, combine the salt and form it into two patties. Then set aside.

2. In a small saucepan, melt the butter and sauté the mushrooms over medium heat, salt and pepper, season and set aside.

3. Meanwhile, add the butter and stir in the flour in a small saucepan; cook for a minute. Slowly whisk in the milk. Bring the sauce up to a simmer and let it thicken. Add the cheese, cayenne and salt to taste; stir well until the cheese melts. Set aside and keep warm.

4. Using a flat top or cast-iron pan, heat the B.B.Q. to 425F. Cook the burgers on each side for 4-6 minutes or until 160-165F is the internal temperature.

5. On the flat top or grill, butter the brioche buns and toast.

6. Place a cheese slice on the bottom of the two buns to assemble the burger, top it with the patty, then the second cheese slice, followed by the bacon, cheese and mushroom sauce, and the top bun.

7. Red Robin Burnin' Love Burger

Preparation time: 30 minutes

Servings: 4

Difficulty: Moderate

Ingredients:

- One tablespoon canola oil
- One teaspoon butter
- One medium thinly sliced onion
- Half teaspoon salt
- ¼ teaspoon black pepper
- Dash salt and Dash sugar
- One pound ground beef
- Four split and toasted hamburger buns
- Two tablespoon crumbled Gorgonzola cheese
- Jalapeno pepper thinly sliced is optional

Instructions:

1. In a small pan heat the oil and butter over medium heat. Add onion, salt and sugar, and cook until deep golden brown. Stirring occasionally 4 to 6 minutes.

2. Mix jelly, salt and pepper in a large bowl, then add the beef and mix lightly but thoroughly. Shape into 4 thick patties.

3. Grill burgers covered, over medium heat four to five minutes on each side. Serve on buns with caramelized onion, cheese and if you desired sliced jalapeno.

8. Red Robin Whiskey River B.B.Q. Burger

Preparation time: 40 minutes

Servings: 6

Difficulty: Moderate

Ingredients:

- Two lbs. of 80/20 ground beef
- Oil, for brushing on burgers
- Six seeded hamburger buns
- Twelve tablespoons of mayonnaise
- Onion Rings - Thin & Crispy
- Bourbon Whiskey B.B.Q. Sauce
- Six slices of Cheddar cheese
- Two cups chopped lettuce
- Twelve slices tomato

Instructions:

1. Preheat a gas grill over high heat or a charcoal grill.
2. Section and shape the ground beef into six patties while the grill preheats. Brush lightly with oil on the burgers.
3. Grill the burgers until browned on the first side and slightly charred (about 3-4 minutes). Flip over the burgers and continue to cook until cooking is desired - about 4 minutes for a medium-rare burger, longer for a more finished burger. Drizzle the Bourbon Whiskey B.B.Q. Burgers with

sauce and place on each burger a slice of cheese. Cook for an extra minute or until the cheese begins to melt. Afterward, remove from the heat and set aside while the burgers are being assembled.

4. To assemble the burger, spread the cut side of both sections of the bun with one tablespoon of mayonnaise on each half to assemble the burger. Place Onion Rings on top of the bottom bun portion of the cut side. With sauce and cheese, add the burger. Top with lettuce and tomatoes. Over the top of a sandwich, replace the top bun. Then serve!

9. Trader Joe's Chili Lime Chicken Burger

Preparation time: 40 minutes

Servings: 4

Difficulty: Moderate

Ingredients:

- One lb. of ground chicken
- Two green onions, chopped
- 1/4 cup chopped red bell pepper
- Two tablespoons chopped cilantro
- Two teaspoons minced garlic
- Half teaspoon salts
- 1/4 teaspoon red pepper flakes
- One lime, cut in half
- Four slices of pepper jack cheese
- Four buns, toasted
- For the guacamole:
- One avocado
- Garlic powder
- Salt & pepper

Instructions:

1. Combine the chicken, green onions, bell pepper, cilantro, garlic, salt, red pepper flakes and half a lime of juice in a large bowl. Mix until they are all fully combined.

---

2. Then, from the combined mixture, form four patties and spray each side with non-stick spray.

3. Over medium-high heat, heat a skillet or a large grill pan.

4. Grill the patties on each side for 3-4 minutes or until they are thoroughly cooked.

5. Place on top of each patty a slice of cheese, then cover it with a large pot lid and let it melt for about a minute.

6. Remove the burgers from the plate, cover with foil, and let stand for 5 minutes. Place a thin toasted bun with each burger, then top with guacamole.

For the guacamole

1. Mash all ingredients together with a potato masher or fork.

10. Nando's Peri Peri Chicken Burgers

Preparation time: 30 minutes

Servings: 4

Difficulty: Moderate

Ingredients:

Peri Peri sauce/marinade

- 1 to 3 birds' eye red chilies (1 is mild, 3 is reasonably spicy). The best substitute is Thai chilis because are small and have the same heat as Birds Eye chilis. Otherwise, dried cayenne pepper is also good substitute (1 teaspoon per birds' eye chili)
- One large red pepper/capsicum
- Five garlic cloves
- Three tablespoon vegetable oil
- Four tablespoon malt vinegar, or any other plain brown vinegar (not balsamic)
- Two tablespoons paprika
- One tablespoon dried oregano
- Two teaspoons onion powder
- One ½ teaspoon white sugar
- One ½ teaspoon salt
- Black pepper to taste
- Few drops of red food colouring, is optional

Pink sauce

- Three tablespoon Peri Peri sauce
- ½ Cup whole egg mayonnaise
- ¼ Cup sour cream or Greek yoghurt

Burgers

- One tablespoon olive oil
- Four chicken thigh fillets (skinless boneless and large enough for a burger)
- Four soft rolls
- Two sliced tomatoes
- Lettuce of choice

Instructions:

1. Place the Peri Peri sauce ingredients in a food processor or blender and whizz until smooth. Pour ½ cup into a bowl with the chicken and let marinate for at least three hours, or up to 24 hours.

2. Mix together three tablespoons of the Peri Peri sauce with the pink sauces ingredients and set aside.

3. Meanwhile, heat one tablespoon of olive oil in a fry pan over medium/high heat or the BBQ. Add the chicken and cook each side for 4 to 5 minutes, or until dark golden brown. Remove from fry pan onto a plate and cover loosely with foil, and allow to rest for five minutes.

4. To make the burgers, split the roll in half and top with lettuce, tomato chicken then pink sauce. If desired drizzle with the residual Peri Peri sauce. Serve with fries.

Chapter 2: Fries and Nachos Recipes

1. T.G.I. Friday's Baked Potato Skins

Preparation time: 45 minutes

Servings: 5

Difficulty: Moderate

Ingredients:

- Ten baked potato halves
- One tablespoon melted butter
- Seasoned salt, to taste
- three-fourth cup shredded Cheddar cheese
- Five strips of cooked and crumbled bacon
- One green onion, diced

Instructions:

1. Preheat the oven to 375 degrees F.
2. Remove as much of the flesh as you can from the potato, leaving only the skin.
3. Brush the butter with the potato shells and season with salt.
4. Bake, until crisp, for 15-20 minutes.
5. Use cheese, bacon, and onion to remove and sprinkle.
6. Place the cheese back in the oven for 6-8 minutes until it is melted.

7. Use sour cream or ranch dressing to serve.

2. Paleo Nachos

Preparation time: 2 hours

Servings: 4

Difficulty: Moderate

Ingredients:

- Two large sweet potatoes, thinly sliced lengthways
- One red onion, finely chopped
- Two garlic cloves, chopped
- one-third cup of extra virgin olive oil
- One red capsicum, finely chopped
- Charred jalapenos for serving
- One small eggplant, finely chopped
- Two teaspoons of dried oregano flakes
- 400g can chopped tomatoes
- 350g lean beef mince
- Coriander leaves to serve
- Two and a half teaspoons of smoked Paprika
- One teaspoon of ground chili
- Two teaspoons of ground cumin
- Half cup (125ml) coconut cream, chilled
- One and a half teaspoons Worcestershire sauce
- Juice of one lime
- Halved avocado for serving

For salsa

- 250g cherry tomatoes, halved
- one-third cup coriander leaves, roughly chopped
- One garlic clove, crushed
- Juice of two limes

Instructions:

1. Preheat the oven to 150 ° C. Place the sweet potatoes in a single layer over three baking trays lined with paper and brush with two tablespoons of oil. Bake for 15 minutes, or until it starts to dry. Bake, turn and swap trays every 15 minutes, for another 1 hour or until crisp, and reduce the oven to 110 ° C. Remove and cool from the oven.

2. Combine the salsa ingredients in a bowl, set aside and season with salt.

3. Heat one tablespoon of oil over medium heat in a large fry-pan. Cook the onion, garlic, and capsicum, or until softened, for 8 minutes. Set aside and remove the onion mixture from the pan.

4. Add the eggplant and one tablespoon of the remaining oil to the pan. Increase the heat to high and cook until tender and golden, or for 8 minutes. Using a slotted spoon, remove the eggplant from the pan and set it aside.

5. Fill the pan with the mince, cumin, chili, oregano and two teaspoons of paprika. Cook for 5 minutes, stirring, or until the meat is browned. Add the tomato, Worcestershire

sauce and two tablespoons (500 ml) of water, then add the onion, garlic, capsicum and eggplant to the bowl. Cook for about 15 minutes or until it is thick and reduced. To taste, season.

6. Meanwhile, in a bowl, combine the coconut cream, lime juice and the rest of the half teaspoon paprika. With salt, season it and set it aside.

7. In a serving dish, arrange sweet potato chips and top with the mixture of spicy beef, charred jalapenos, avocado, coriander, tomato salsa, and coconut cream dressing.

3. Chi Chi's Seafood Nachos

Preparation time: 45 minutes

Servings: 2

Difficulty: Moderate

Ingredients:

- 16 large tortilla chips
- One package of Louis Kemp Crab Delights
- One thawed frozen package of salad shrimp
- One package of Louis Kemp Lobster Delights
- One cup of shredded Monterey jack cheese

Instructions:

1. Spread on a ten-inch plate with tortilla chips.

2. Over the chips, layer the crab, lobster, and shrimps.

3. Sprinkle on top of the cheese.

4. Microwave for one and a half to two and a half minutes, on medium, until melted.

4. Taco Bell Nacho Fries

Preparation time: 30 minutes

Servings: 2

Difficulty: Moderate

Ingredients:

- One large Russet Potato, cut into 1/2 fries
- One tablespoon Olive Oil, divided
- Two teaspoons Chili Powder
- One teaspoon Garlic Powder
- One teaspoon Dried Oregano
- 1/4 teaspoon Kosher Salt
- 1/4 teaspoon Ground Coriander
- 1-2 Tablespoon Cheddar Powder, optional

Cheese Dipping Sauce

- 1/2 Cup Fat Free Greek Yogurt
- Two Tablespoon Taco Sauce
- Two Tablespoon Cheddar Powder

Instructions:

1. Wash and dry the potato before cutting it into 1/2 fries. Pat dry with a paper towel and add to a large bowl with 1/2 Tablespoon olive oil. Toss to coat and add to an air fryer basket.
2. Air fry for 20 minutes at 400°F or until the fries begin to turn golden brown. While the fries cook, mix the spices and cheddar powder together in a small bowl.

3. After the fries have cooked, add them back to the large bowl and toss with the remaining olive oil before adding 3/4 of the spice blend. Toss/stir well to evenly coat the fries.

4. Add the fries back to the air fryer or oven for another 3-5 minutes until crispy. Be careful not to burn them! Transfer back to the bowl and toss with the remaining spices/cheddar powder.

5. Mix the cheese sauce ingredients together and serve with warm fries. Enjoy!

5. Tex Mex Nachos Recipe

Preparation time: 20 minutes

Servings: 5

Difficulty: Moderate

Ingredients:

- ¾ lb ground beef
- ¾ Cup mild salsa
- ¼ teaspoon garlic powder
- Seven oz can pinto beans, drained
- Seven oz can whole corn kernel, drained
- Three large tortilla, baked into the chips
- Three cups shredded lettuce
- One cup small sliced dices tomato
- Two cups shredded cheddar cheese
- ½ Cup sliced black olives
- ½ Cup sliced pickled jalapenos
- ½ Cup sour cream
- ½ Cup guacamole
- Salt and ground black pepper to taste

Instructions:

1. Preheat the oven to 400 F.

2. Heat some oil in a pan over medium heat, and begin cooking the green onions and meat.

3. When the meat mixture is cooked, remove and drain the excess oil and return then into the same pan.

4. Add the mild salsa, garlic powder, beans and corn, and saute briefly.

5. Adjust with salt and pepper, and set aside.

6. Arrange the chips on a oven safe tray or plate.

7. Add some spoon of the meat mixture onto the chips, and then add on the lettuce, tomatoes, cheese, olives and jalapenos.

8.Place the entire tray into the oven and bake it for 1-2 minutes until the cheese has melted.

9. Remove from the oven, add sour cream and guacamole (if using) on top of it and serve hot. Enjoy!

6. Outback Steakhouse Blooming Onion

Preparation time: 2 hours 10 minutes

Servings: 1

Difficulty: Moderate

Ingredients:

Batter:

- Four Vidalia or Texas Sweet Onions
- One-third cup cornstarch
- One and a half cups flour
- Two teaspoons garlic, minced
- Two teaspoons Paprika
- One teaspoon salt
- One teaspoon pepper
- 24 oz. beer
- Seasoned Flour
- Two cups flour
- Four teaspoons Paprika
- Two teaspoons garlic powder
- Half teaspoon peppers
- 1/4 teaspoon cayenne pepper

Creamy Chili Sauce:

- One-pint Mayonnaise
- One-pint Sour cream
- Half cup chili sauce

- Half teaspoon cayenne pepper

Instructions:

1. Until well blended, mix the cornstarch, flour, and seasonings.
2. Mix well, add beer.
3. "Cut off the top of the onion and peel about 3/4 ". Cut into 12 to 16 vertical wedges of onion, but do not cut through the bottom root.
4. Take about 1 inch of petals out of the center of the onion. Dip the onion into the seasoned flour and shake away the excess.
5. Separate the petals and dip to thoroughly coat them in the batter. Place gently in the fryer basket and deep-fry for one and a half minutes at 375 F to 400 F.
6. Turn over, and fry for one and a half more minute.
7. Drain on towels made of paper.
8. Place the onion upright in a shallow bowl and use a circular cutter or apple corer to remove the center core. With Creamy Chili Sauce, serve hot.

Chapter 3: Sweet Cookies and Ice-Cream Recipes

1. Auntie Anne's Soft Pretzels

Preparation time: 55 minutes

Servings: 12

Difficulty: Moderate

Ingredients:

- One and a half cups of warm water
- One and 1/8 teaspoons of active dry yeast
- Two tablespoons of brown sugar
- One and 1/8 teaspoons of salt
- One cup of bread flour
- Three cups of regular flour
- Two cups of warm water
- Two tablespoons of baking soda
- Coarse salt as per taste
- Four tablespoons of melted butter

Instructions:

1. Preheat the oven to 400 degrees F.
2. Add water to a mixing cup and sprinkle it with yeast. Stir to dissolve.
3. Add the salt and brown sugar and whisk to dissolve.

4. The flour is added, and when smooth and elastic, the dough is kneaded.

5. For at least half an hour, let the dough stretch.

6. When the dough is rising, make a baking soda water bath with two cups of water and two teaspoons of baking soda. Make sure to stir occasionally.

7. After the dough has risen, pinch away bits of dough and roll it into a long rope shape.

8. Dip each pretzel in the soda solution and place it on the oiled baking sheet.

9. Let the pretzels rise. Sprinkle coarse salt on it.

10. Bake them in the oven for about 10 minutes, or until crispy. Brush and serve with butter that is melted.

2. McDonald's Creme Egg Mc Flurry

Preparation time: 10 minutes

Servings: 2

Difficulty: Easy

Ingredients:

- Three and a half Cups of Vanilla Ice Cream
- 1/4 Cup of Milk
- Three Cadbury Creme Eggs
- Half Cup of Chocolate Chips

Instructions:

1. Unwrap the Cadbury Creme Eggs and cut them altogether. Divide the eggs that were smashed in half and set them aside.
2. Crush the chocolate chips or chop them up and set them aside.
3. Blend your preference for vanilla ice cream and milk.
4. Thirty seconds before the completion of mixing, add in half of the milk eggs and mix for 30 more seconds.
5. Empty the ice cream contents into two cups or bowls and fold them into the smashed chocolate chips.
6. Sprinkle on top of all sweets with the second half of the creme eggs.
7. Immediately, enjoy your homemade Creme Egg Mc Flurry!

3. Subway White Chocolate Macadamia Nut Cookies

Preparation time: 1 hour 15 minutes

Servings: 16

Difficulty: Hard

Ingredients:

- 150g plain flour
- One egg
- 115g unsalted butter
- Half teaspoon of salt
- Half teaspoon of bicarbonate of soda
- One teaspoon of vanilla extract
- 150g caster sugar
- 225g white chocolate
- 185g chopped macadamia nuts

Instructions:

1. Preheat to 180 ° C / Gas Mark 4 in your oven.
2. In a medium-large mixing dish, blend the butter and sugar until they are smooth.
3. Then stir in the egg, beating until well blended.
4. Add the vanilla and stir, then add the rice, salt and baking soda, stirring regularly.

5. Apply the white chocolate and macadamia nuts to the mixture until fully mixed and stir until blended.

6. Place the cookie dough inside a baking tray on baking sheets and divide the space equally between them.

7. Bake for about 8 minutes in the oven until well browned. Remove the cookies slightly until they appeared wholly baked, as they would begin to heat themselves until withdrawn from the oven.

8. Wait until frozen, then enjoy white chocolate macadamia nut cookies of your Subway quality!

4. Payday Candy Bars

Preparation time: 45 minutes
Servings: Eight
Difficulty: Moderate

Ingredients:

- Five caramel squares
- 1/4 cup milk
- One teaspoon of peanut butter
- One tablespoon of corn syrup
- Half teaspoon of vanilla
- Half teaspoon of salt
- One and 1/4 cups of powdered sugar
- 20 caramel squares
- One tablespoon of water
- Two cups of dry roasted peanuts (slightly crushed)

Instructions:

1. In a saucepan, combine the first six ingredients. Cook until the caramel has melted and stirs easily, over low heat. To blend in, add 3/4 cup powdered sugar and stir.
2. Reserve the sugar that exists.
3. Switch to the medium-high sun. Cook the caramel mixture until precisely 230F using a sugar thermometer, thus

stirring constantly. Remove from fire, let cool and add the remaining powdered sugar for a few minutes.

4. Beat in the sugar for a few minutes with a hand mixer. For 20 minutes, let the candy cool.

5. Divide eight similar pieces of candy and turn each into 4-inch logs. Place on paper with wax and let cool for an hour.

6. Add the excess caramel and water to a double boiler. Melt until it is smooth. Remove from the heat, but keep hot water under the caramel to not firm up. Cover one of the logs with molten caramel using a pastry brush.

7. Roll with peanuts in a small bowl. If some spots are not fully coated with peanuts, add more caramel and stick to the peanuts again. With the remaining logs, repeat.

8. Enable it to absolutely cool before feeding.

5. Clark Bars

Preparation time: 45 minutes

Servings: 1

Difficulty: Moderate

Ingredients:

- One (16 ounces) package of graham crackers, crumbled
- One cup of melted butter
- Two and a half cups of peanut butter
- Two and a half cups of confectioners' sugar
- Two cups of semi-sweet chocolate chips
- One (14 ounces) can have sweetened condensed milk

Instructions:

1. Oil a 9x13 inch pan. Combine the graham cracker crumbs, honey, peanut butter and powdered sugar in a large mixing bowl.
2. Press the mixture in the prepared pan. In a small kettle, melt the chocolate chips and condensed milk together on low heat. Stir until it's mixed properly.
3. Spread it with the chocolate mixture over the peanut butter mixture. Refrigerate the cookie bars for 4 hours.
4. Slice and eat.

6. Dairy Queen Ice Cream

Preparation Time: 2 hours 10 minutes

Servings: 12

Difficulty: Moderate

Ingredients:

- Two envelopes of Knox gelatin
- ½ Cup cold water
- Four cups whole milk
- Two cups of sugar
- Two teaspoons vanilla extract
- ½ Teaspoon salt
- Three cups cream

Instructions:

1. In cold water, soak Knox gelatin. Heat your milk, but don't boil it.
2. Remove it from the heat and add the gelatin, sugar, vanilla extract, and salt. Refrigerate it, and then add the ice cream. Afterward, for 5 to 6 hours, refrigerate and then savor.
3. Pour in a 4 to 6-quart freezer of ice cream. Then process it as per the instructions of the manufacturer.

Chapter 4: Snack Recipes

1.Panda Expresses' Chow Mein

Preparation time: 1 hour

Servings: 1

Difficulty: Moderate

Ingredients:

- One tablespoon vegetable oil
- Two green onions, trimmed and cut crosswise into ½-inch-thick pieces
- a quarter cup sliced celery
- One and a half cups sliced Napa cabbage
- a quarter cup bean sprout
- a quarter teaspoon sugar
- Half cup chicken broth
- One and a half teaspoons soy sauce
- One teaspoon Asian sesame oil
- One and a half teaspoons cornstarch, dissolved in one tablespoon cold water
- Four ounces thin whole-grain noodles, cooked according to the package Instructions
- Red pepper flakes

Instructions:

1. Heat the oil in a wok or large skillet and stir-fry the green onions, celery, cabbage, and bean sprouts for about three minutes, or until the cabbage is wilted. Add the sugar, broth, soy sauce, sesame oil, and simmer, covered, for 3 minutes.

2. Stir in the mixture of cornstarch and water and bring the wok contents to a boil—the sauce will thicken.

3. Serve over the whole grain noodles and season with red pepper flakes.

2. Panda Expresses' Garlic Chicken breasts with String Beans

Preparation time: 1 hour

Servings: 4

Difficulty: Moderate

Ingredients:

- Two tablespoons soy sauce
- Two teaspoons rice wine vinegar
- One teaspoon Asian sesame oil
- Two teaspoons cornstarch
- One teaspoon sugar
- One pound of boneless, skinless chicken breasts, cut into 1⁄4-inch strips
- Two tablespoons vegetable oil
- One large onion, peeled and cut into 1⁄2-inch wedges
- Two tablespoons minced garlic
- One teaspoon black bean sauce
- 12 ounces green beans, cut into 3-inch pieces
- One cup coarsely diced red bell pepper
- Hot cooked rice or noodles, for serving

Instructions:

1. Combine the rice wine vinegar, sesame oil, cornstarch and sugar with the soy sauce. To mix all the ingredients, whisk.

To cover properly, apply the chicken strips and toss. Refrigerate for about 20 minutes, sealed.

2. In a wok or large skillet, heat the vegetable oil and fry the chicken for around 3 minutes or until the chicken starts to brown and is cooked through. Take the fried chicken out of the wok and keep it warm.

3. Add the onion, garlic, and black bean sauce to the same wok. Add the green beans and bell pepper easily.

4. Add a quarter cup of sugar, cover and cook for 3 minutes or until the vegetables are soft and crisp. Put the chicken back into the wok and easily stir-fry to mix the flavors. Serve over rice or noodles.

3. Panda Expresses' Spicy Chicken

Preparation time: 1 hour
Servings: 1
Difficulty: Moderate

Ingredients:

- Half cup diced chayote squash
- Half cup vegetable oil
- 12 ounces chicken, diced
- Salt and black pepper
- One-third cup diced onion
- A quarter cup diced red bell pepper
- Eight pieces whole dried chile pepper
- Half teaspoon minced fresh ginger
- Half teaspoon minced garlic
- One and a half teaspoons red pepper flakes, or to taste
- Half teaspoon Shao Hosing wine
- One teaspoon soy sauce
- Two tablespoons chicken broth
- One teaspoon sugar
- Dash of Asian sesame oil
- One tablespoon cornstarch
- A quarter cup roasted peanut

—

Instructions:

1. Blanch the diced chayote for a minute in a steamer or boiling water, then drain and set aside.

2. Heat a quarter cup of the vegetable oil in a wok or skillet and add the chicken, seasoned with salt and black pepper.

3. Stir-fry until cooked through, then add the onion and bell pepper and cook until the vegetables are crisp-tender.

4. Drain the vegetables with the chicken and set them aside.

5. In the same wok, heat the remaining a quarter cup oil and stir-fry the chile pepper, ginger, and garlic until slightly soft. Add the red pepper flakes, Shao Hosing wine, soy sauce, chicken broth, sugar, and sesame oil. Bring to a boil and whisk in the cornstarch.

6. Add the cooked chicken mixture and blanched chayote and toss with the other ingredients to combine. Toss in the peanuts and serve warm.

4. Starbucks Tarragon Chicken Salad

Preparation time: 40 minutes

Servings: 2

Difficulty: Moderate

Ingredients:

- a quarter cup mayonnaise
- One tablespoon fresh chopped tarragon
- One teaspoon lemon juice
- 2 cups ½" cubed cooked chicken
- a quarter cup finely chopped dried cranberries
- One stalk finely chopped celery
- One tablespoon finely chopped red onion

Instructions:

1. In a small bowl, create the dressing by combining the mayonnaise, tarragon and lemon juice. Mix well.
2. In a medium bowl, add the chicken, cranberries, celery, and onion and lightly toss to mix.
3. Add the dressing and mix well.

5. Subway Orchard Chicken Salad

Preparation time: 40 minutes

Servings: 4

Difficulty: Moderate

Ingredients:

- A quarter cup plain nonfat yogurt
- Two tablespoons light mayonnaise
- Two teaspoons lemon juice
- Half teaspoon sugar
- One cup cubed cooked chicken breast
- Half cup diced celery
- One cup chopped red apples
- A quarter cup golden raisins or white grapes
- A quarter cup dried cranberries or cherries

Instructions:

1. Make the salad dressing in a small bowl by mixing the yogurt, mayonnaise, lemon juice, and sugar.
2. Add the rest of the ingredients to a large bowl.
3. Pour the yogurt mixture over the chicken mixture. Toss well to mix.
4. Cover and chill for at least 2 hours.

6. Subway Veggie Delight Wrap

Preparation time: 40 minutes

Servings: 1

Difficulty: Moderate

Ingredients:

- A quarter cup refried bean
- One slice of cheese of your choice
- One whole-wheat tortilla
- Half cup shredded lettuce
- Half cup diced tomato
- A quarter cup diced onion
- Four pickle slices
- Three diced olives
- Two teaspoons fat-free Italian salad dressing
- Two teaspoons honey mustard salad dressing

Instructions:

1. Spread the refried beans and cheese onto the tortilla.
2. Place on a plate and microwave for 30–60 seconds, until the cheese melts.
3. Add the vegetables, pickles, and olives on top of the melted cheese.
4. Drizzle the salad dressings on top of the vegetables.
5. Roll up like a burrito.

7. Subway Sweet Onion Chicken Teriyaki Sandwich

Preparation time: 50 minutes

Servings: 1

Difficulty: Moderate

Ingredients:

- One boneless, skinless chicken breast
- A quarter cup Lawry's teriyaki marinade
- One bakery-fresh sub roll
- Sliced vegetables of your choice
- Sweet Onion Sauce
- Half cup light corn syrup
- One tablespoon red wine vinegar
- One tablespoon minced white onion
- Two tablespoons white vinegar
- One teaspoon brown sugar
- One teaspoon balsamic vinegar
- A quarter teaspoon lemon juice
- 1/8 teaspoon salt
- 1/8 teaspoon poppy seeds
- Pinch of cracked black pepper
- Pinch of garlic powder

Instructions:

1. Place and marinate the chicken breast in a zip-top bag. In the refrigerator, marinate the chicken for 30 minutes.

2. In a shallow microwave-safe dish, combine all the sauce ingredients. Heat until the mixture boils for 1–2 minutes.

3. Stir thoroughly, cover and let cool.

4. On a George Foreman barbecue or stovetop grill pan, cook the chicken. Cut into slices of 1/4''.

5. Place the chicken on the roll of a subway. Whatever veggies you like, add them.

6. Pour over the chicken and vegetables with the hot onion sauce.

8. T.G.I. Friday's Strawberry Fields Salad

Preparation time: 1 hour

Servings: 2

Difficulty: Moderate

Ingredients:

Glazed Pecans

- One cup chopped pecans
- A quarter cup dark brown sugar
- One tablespoon water
- Strawberry Glaze
- 12 strawberries
- A quarter cup balsamic vinegar
- A quarter cup granulated sugar
- Two tablespoons water

Salad

- One head red leaf lettuce
- One head of romaine lettuce
- Two ounces of shredded Parmesan cheese
- Six ounces of balsamic vinaigrette dressing
- Cracked pepper, to taste

Instructions:

1. Mix the sliced pecans with brown sugar and water in a shallow sauté pan over medium heat. For 4-5 minutes, cook. Only put aside.

2. Break the strawberries into slices of 1/4"

3. Mix the vinegar, sugar, and water with the sliced strawberries in a shallow cup. And put aside.

4. Chop the lettuces into 2" bits.

5. Place the broccoli, parmesan, vinaigrette, and pecans in a wide dish.

6. From the glaze, strain the strawberries and put them on top of the salad. Apply to the end of the salad, the crushed black pepper.

9. KFC Popcorn Chicken

Preparation time: 20 minutes

Servings: 4

Difficulty: Easy

Ingredients:

- 300 grams of boneless chicken fillets
- Half teaspoon of paprika
- Half teaspoon of onion powder
- Two tablespoons of corn flour
- One large egg
- One cup of bread crumbs
- Half teaspoon of Garlic powder
- A Pinch of pepper
- A Pinch of salt

Instructions:

1. Begin by cutting the fillets of chicken into little popcorn-sized bites.
2. For a few minutes, soak each piece of chicken in the egg.
3. Put a pinch of pepper, a pinch of salt, paprika, garlic powder, onion powder and
   corn flour in a small pan as the chicken soaks.
4. Remove the chicken parts from the egg mixture and leave to soak off the extra mixture on a paper towel for a few minutes.

5. Then roll the mixture of herbs, spices and flour with each popcorn chicken bite. On both sides, cover each section well.

6. Directly extract each piece of chicken from the herb mixture and roll in the breadcrumbs.

7. Set each piece aside as you heat the oil for a few minutes. This will allow the bread to stick well to the chicken.

8. We prefer a small tabletop fryer for frying, so we can also sear on both sides. Make sure that the oil is about 175°C (350°F).

9. Drop-in the fryer with a few bits of popcorn chicken and cook on both sides until golden brown. Turn periodically! To ensure that the chicken is fried, we fry each piece for 4-5 minutes.

10. Remove each batch from the fryer and allow it to cool before enjoying it on a few sheets of paper!

10. McDonald's Chicken Nuggets

Preparation time: 1 hour 15 minutes

Servings: 10 to 12

Difficulty: Moderate

Ingredients:

- Four chicken breast fillets
- One cup of water
- One cup of all-purpose flour
- One tablespoon of onion powder
- Two tablespoons of salt
- Vegetable oil
- One egg
- 1/4 tablespoon of black pepper
- 1/6 tablespoon of garlic powder
- Half tablespoon of MSG

Instructions:

1. You get to unleash a little rage with this first move by pounding and squashing each breast fillet!
2. When each fillet is around a quarter of an inch in height, the chicken breast fillets are sliced into smaller, manageable pieces.
3. Beat the egg in a small bowl and pour in a cup of water.

4. Next, put the rice, salt, pepper, onion powder, garlic powder and MSG in a small food bag and pour it in. When one of the mixtures were in the bag, giving it a fair shake.

5. Now is the time to blend the flour mixture with each chicken slice. Do this by just putting each nugget in the bag and shaking it a little. Do one or two at a time for this.

6. Remove the pieces of meat, place them and cover well in the egg mixture.

7. For a final shake, then return the coated chicken parts to the bag.

8. When all the nuggets are well coated, put them for about an hour in the refrigerator.

9. Some people now want to add another coating to the chicken bites after refrigerating them. We didn't bother with this move, but if you have leftovers, give them another whirl in the egg and then the flour mixture!

10. Now make sure you preheat the oil to around 370 °F (185 °C) in a tabletop fryer.

11. For about 10 minutes, put the nuggets in the fryer, rotating once. At this stage, remember not to overload the fryer!

12. Take the nuggets out of the fryer and leave them to drain for a few minutes in a paper bag (or sheet of paper).

13. Serve and eat until all of the nuggets have been fried and drained!

Chapter 5: Sauces, Slaws and Dips Recipes

1. Arby's Barbecue Sauce

Preparation time: 35 minutes
Servings: 1 cup
Difficulty: Moderate

Ingredients:
- One cup ketchup
- Two teaspoons water
- Two teaspoons brown sugar
- Half teaspoon Worcestershire sauce
- Half teaspoon Tabasco sauce
- A quarter teaspoon onion powder
- A quarter teaspoon garlic powder
- A quarter teaspoon salt
- A quarter teaspoon pepper

Instructions:
1. Combine in a shallow saucepan all the ingredients. Set over medium heat.
2. Stir continuously until it boils with the sauce.
3. For 7-10 minutes, cook.
4. Remove from the heat and leave to cool off.

2. McDonald's Tartar Sauce

Preparation time: 45 minutes

Servings: 12

Difficulty: Moderate

Ingredients:

- One cup mayonnaise
- One teaspoon sugar
- Two teaspoons dill pickle relish
- Three teaspoons white onion finely chopped

Instructions:

1. Combine in a shallow bowl all ingredients.
2. Cover and allow to rest before serving for at least 30 minutes.
3. Place it in your refrigerator in an airtight container.

3. Big Mac Sauce

Preparation time: 45 minutes
Servings: 4
Difficulty: Moderate

Ingredients:
- 1/4 cup Miracle Whip
- 1/4 cup mayonnaise
- Two tablespoons of French salad dressing
- Half tablespoons of sweet relish
- Two teaspoons dill pickle relish
- One teaspoon sugar
- One teaspoon dried, minced onion
- One teaspoon white vinegar
- One teaspoon ketchup
- 1/8 teaspoon salt

Instructions:
1. Mix and allow flavors to blend for about an hour before using.

4. KFC Zinger Sauce

Preparation time: 10 minutes

Servings: 2

Difficulty: Easy

Ingredients:

- Four tablespoons of Tomato ketchup
- Two tablespoons of mayonnaise
- One tablespoon of Vinegar
- Two tablespoons of Chilli Garlic Sauce
- A pinch of Salt
- Half tablespoon of Crushed Red Chilli

Instructions:

1. Mix Tomato Ketchup, Mayonnaise, Chilli Garlic Sauce, Vinegar and a pinch of salt in a bowl.
2. If you have a better spice tolerance, you can add a small amount of crushed Red Chilli to it.

5. Subway Chipotle Sauce

Preparation time: 30 minutes

Servings: 4 to 6

Difficulty: Easy

Ingredients:

- 3/4 cup of mayonnaise
- One ounce of chipotle chile in adobo sauce
- 1/4 ounce of fresh garlic
- A half-ounce of fresh lime juice
- A half-ounce of Dijon mustard
- A pinch of salt

Instructions:

1. Put the chipotle chili in a food processor and then add one tablespoon of adobo sauce from the chipotle can.
2. Put all the other ingredients in the chipotle blender and gently season with salt.
3. Whizz the sauce up and mix until the consistency is flawless. A strong blast of two or 3 minutes will do the job and make the mixture gorgeous and smooth.
4. Empty the food blender's South West sauce into a small bowl and put it in the fridge. Before cooking your sandwich, leave for at least 30 minutes, then indulge!

CHAPTER 6: Beverages Recipes

1. McDonald's Vanilla Iced Coffee

Preparation time: 25 minutes
Servings: 6
Difficulty: Easy

Ingredients:

- Six tablespoons ground coffee
- Six and one-third cups cold water
- 14 ounces sweetened condensed milk
- Two tablespoons vanilla extract
- Ice cubes

Instructions:

1. Brew the coffee in a coffee maker. After it's done brewing, set it aside to cool.
2. Combine both the brewed coffee and sweetened condensed milk in a large pitcher.
3. Stir thoroughly until coffee, and condensed milk are blended.
4. Stir in the vanilla extract.
5. Refrigerate until the coffee is chilled.
6. Serve in glasses filled with ice.

2. Sonic Cherry Limeade

Preparation time: 20 minutes

Servings: 1

Difficulty: Easy

Ingredients:

- One (12-ounce) can of Sprite
- Juice of three lime wedges
- A quarter cup cherry juice

Instructions:

1. Fill a 2/3 full 16-ounce glass with ice. Over the cold, pour the Sprite.
2. Squeeze in the drink with the lime juice and add the wedges in.
3. Add the juice from the cherry.
4. With a straw, serve.

3. Starbucks Coffee Frappe

Preparation time: 25 minutes

Servings: 2

Difficulty: Easy

Ingredients:

- 18–22 crushed ice cubes
- Seven ounces chilled double-strength coffee
- Two tablespoons granulated sugar
- Two tablespoons flavored syrup of choice
- Whipped cream for garnish

Instructions:

1. Put the ice, coffee, sugar, and syrup in a blender.
2. Blend until a smooth mixture is formed.
3. Pour into a large, tall glass.
4. Afterward, garnish with whipped cream.

4. Starbucks Mocha Frappucino

Preparation time: 25 minutes

Servings: 4

Difficulty: Easy

Ingredients:

- Six cups double-strength brewed dark roast coffee
- Two cups nonfat milk
- 2/3 cup unsweetened cocoa powder
- Cocoa powder, for garnish

Instructions:

1. Cover half of the blended coffee with ice cube trays and put them in the fridge.
2. Mix the remaining brewed coffee, cocoa powder, and milk in a bowl and stir well until dissolved.
3. Chill and cover.
4. Move them to a zip-top bag when the ice cubes have hardened, then crush them.
5. Cover the crushed ice with four glasses and equally split the coffee-cocoa mixture between them. With cocoa powder, dust the top of each bottle.

5. Orange Julius

Preparation time: 20 minutes

Servings: 1

Difficulty: Easy

Ingredients:

- Six ounces of frozen orange juice concentrate
- One cup of milk
- One cup of water
- A quarter cup sugar
- One teaspoon vanilla
- Eight ice cubes

Instructions:

1. Blend all the ingredients mentioned above except for the ice cubes in the blender.
2. Blend in for 1-2 minutes.
3. One at a time, add ice cubes and blend until smooth.

6. Wendy's Frosty

Preparation time: 20 minutes

Servings: 2 to 4

Difficulty: Easy

Ingredients:

- Three-fourth cup milk
- A quarter cup Hershey chocolate powder
- Four cups vanilla ice cream

Instructions:

1. Blend all of the above ingredients for the cocktail in a mixer.
2. Blend until smooth and dense at medium speed. If needed, stir.
3. For too thin, in the serving cups, freeze the mixture until it is thicker.

7. Starbucks Caramel Frappuccino

Preparation time: 10 minutes

Servings: Two

Difficulty: Easy

Ingredients:

- One cup of strongly brewed coffee
- Half cup of milk
- Half cup of caramel syrup
- One cup of large ice cubes
- Two tablespoons of granulated sugar
- Caramel sauce to serve with
- Whipped cream to serve with

Instructions:

1. Start by applying to the food blender a cup of deeply brewed coffee, ensuring it is cold beforehand.
2. Then add the milk, white sugar, caramel syrup, and ice cubes. Blend all the ingredients until a good smooth mixture is obtained; let's say, for about 30 seconds.
3. Pour it into a bowl and finish with whipped cream and syrup.

8. McDonald's Shamrock Shake

Preparation time: 5 minutes

Servings: 1

Difficulty: Easy

Ingredients:

- One cup of whole milk
- Two large scoops of vanilla ice cream
- One teaspoon of peppermint extract
- Three drops of green food colouring
- Whipped cream

Instructions:

1. All the ingredients are to be put into a blender.
2. Blend until you get your desired consistency
3. Pour the shake into a lovely glass of dessert and finish with as much whipped cream as your fancy requires.
4. Enjoy.

9. Dunkin Donuts Coffee Coolatta

Preparation time: 5 minutes

Servings: 1

Difficulty: Easy

Ingredients:

- Six to seven Coffee Ice Cubes
- Two-third Cup of Coffee
- One tablespoon of sugar
- Two-third Cup of Whole Milk or Light Cream
- Whipped Cream

Instructions:

1. The night before, begin by freezing your coffee into iced cubes. You can always use regular iced cubes if you don't have the time or fancy a Coolatta within the next 5 minutes.
2. Put the iced cubes into a blender once you have them. (coffee or regular).
3. Along with the sugar, pour the cup of coffee into the blender.
4. Now, add the whole milk or light cream and blend it until you get a slushy mixture for about 2 minutes.
5. Pour the mixture of coffee into a tall glass and top it with whipped cream.

10. Shake Shack's Peanut Butter Shake

Preparation time: 5 minutes

Servings: 3

Difficulty: Easy

Ingredients:

- One cup milk
- Two cups Vanilla ice cream
- Half cup Peanut butter
- Two tablespoon sugar

Instructions:

1. Combine all ingredients in a blender; cover and process for 30 seconds or until smooth. Stir if necessary and pour into chilled glasses. Serve immediately.

Conclusion

I'm very glad you've taken the time to read this book. I hope that with regards to Fast food Copycat recipes, all your questions are clear.

It is about learning the restaurants' simple ingredients and techniques to make the masterpiece dish to create a copycat recipe.

Creating a copy of the popular dish also allows you to adjust the ingredients used according to your tastes and health restrictions to produce a custom recipe.

It is also a cost-effective way to eat popular meals that you want. Keep cooking and try to work with the recipes.

Well, thanks and good luck!